Instagram Marketing

Using Instagram to Skyrocket your Business Rapidly

ABOUT THE AUTHOR

George Pain is an entrepreneur, author and engineer. He specializes in setting up online businesses from scratch, investment income strategies and global mobility solutions. He has successfully built several businesses from the ground up and is excited to share his knowledge with you.

DISCLAIMER

Table of Contents

Introduction

Launched in 2010, Instagram is a social networking app that allows users to share photos and videos using their handheld devices such as smartphones or tablet devices. Like Facebook or Twitter, you can create your own Instagram account and watch content through your newsfeed. If you post pictures or videos on the app, these will be shown on your profile.

The app showed so much potential that Facebook bought it just 18 months after its launch through an acquisition deal worth $1 Billion. What's even more impressive is that the platform has sustained its expected growth.

Recent data from *statista.com* reveals that Instagram is now the second most popular social networking app in the United States. As of February 2018, the app recorded more than 106.17 million monthly users. If you need to market your business to people who are likely using Instagram, you should add this platform to your marketing channels.

Whether you are in charge of managing the social media channels of a large company or a small business, or even if you're simply trying to grow your personal brand, adding Instagram into your digital strategy is a must!

With this beginner's guide, you can learn the fundamentals of marketing your business through Instagram. Specifically, we will tackle the following topics:

- The primary advantages of using Instagram
- Knowing whether Instagram is right for your business
- Defining your ideal Instagram followers
- Growing your brand through Instagram engagement
- Developing your content on Instagram
- How to use Instagram to boost your sales
- And many more!

Like most technological platforms, Instagram is still evolving. And before you can keep up, you should start discovering this mobile app and how it can bring magic to your marketing efforts.

The Benefits of Using Instagram

Marketing is primarily about connecting with your customers to change the way they think or behave so you can influence them to do a specific action. The best way to really invoke this change in perception is to dominate where your customers are spending their time. And as already pointed out in the Introduction, Instagram is one of the most popular social networking apps today.

In general, Instagram can help you grow your brand online, post engaging content, nurture the relationship with your customers, evaluate your marketing performance, and boost your sales.

Improve Brand Awareness through Instagram

One secret to effective marketing is great storytelling. We love stories because it's part of our nature. From a business viewpoint, telling a great story is one amazing way to invoke an emotional connection with your customers.

With Instagram, you can tell great stories by sharing visual content. In one engaging picture or video, you can invite your audience to enter your world, allowing them to know what you are building or what you could offer.

Gone are the days when marketing is all about the features of products. Today, the effective approach is focused on the customer. Hence, it is crucial not to use Instagram as a platform to showcase your products or services. Rather, you should focus your efforts on human emotions. Instagram is most effective if you use it to encourage an emotional response for your brand.

Instagram is a visual-focused app, and it is one of the main reasons behind its success. Images are the most-engaging content today. In fact, *webdam.com* reveals that visual posts generate 650% higher engagement compared to posts that only contain text. Adding more visual elements to your marketing will not only allow your target customer to easily understand your message, it also enables better recall for your brand.

You can use Instagram to check what resonates with your target customers in the visual context. This will help you improve your branding across channels, and you can also use the visuals you use on Instagram on your other marketing platforms such as your email newsletters or blog.

The best practices in brand development and promotion still apply when it comes to Instagram marketing. Basically, you need to define your target audience and brand personality that will encourage your followers to consider you as a member of their community. You can learn more about this in Chapter 3.

Instagram Is Essential for Your Content Marketing

Instagram, specifically Instagram Stories, can provide great benefits for your content marketing strategy. In a 2017 report from CNBC, Instagram Stories has crushed Snapchat with its 250 million daily active users. This is way higher compared to Snapchat's 166 million daily users in June last year. Clearly, Instagram Stories have already surpassed Snapchat in the market of vanishing content, which is an impressive development for the social media app.

Every time you post a story on your Instagram account, your profile will appear on top of the screen. With the social media app's algorithm, your profile will instantly show stories that users could view and interact with first. It is crucial that you regularly post your stories so you stay current on feeds and improve your brand visibility.

Another great benefit of using Instagram Stories is that you can really use your creative juices and post a variety of content. Instagram Stories will allow you to improve your content with filters, text, stickers, and colors. From boomerangs, short video clips, and photos, you can easily create all the content you want so you can better encourage engagement from your target audience. Read Chapter 4 to learn more about how you can develop a content strategy that is suitable for your followers on Instagram.

Win More Fans and Ambassadors on Instagram

Building a fanbase is a cornerstone of marketing your business online. This will allow you to build a large group of people who will help you exponentially grow your audience who will rave about your brand.

Before you can even sell your products or services, you should first make certain that you have a large following online. It makes it so easy to sell anything if you have a large fanbase who already trust you and are ready to buy.

Instagram is one of the best platforms for growing your fanbase. Aside from the popularity of the platform, the infrastructure makes it easy for businesses to engage with their audience, helping them nurture the relationship. In Chapter 5, we will explore the best strategies to grow a massive following on Instagram.

Boost Your Sales through Instagram

Most people who are using Instagram are shoppers. In a 2017 study conducted by Dana Rebecca Designs, Instagram influences around 75% of user purchase decisions. The report also noted that of 2,000 Instagrammers surveyed, 85% are following accounts that centered on fashion, art, and lifestyle.

When you post the right content on Instagram, your followers will absorb the message without any hard pitch from your end. It works like magic because you can influence your customers without directly telling them to buy from you.

It is now a norm for customers to search online for references before they buy. This includes social media presence. The most popular social media platforms such as Instagram can help you convert your prospects into actual paying customers.

There are specific tactics you can do with your Instagram marketing, and you can learn the most effective methods in Chapter 6.

You Can Outsource and Automate Your Marketing

Instagram marketing is not rocket science. You don't need to earn a degree or undergo rigorous training before you can effectively use it to market your business online. Hence, you can easily do it on your own. There are plenty of resources you can read such as blogs, video tutorials, eBooks, and forums where you can learn the latest strategies that bring real results.

However, not everyone can take Instagram marketing as a do-it-yourself endeavor. For example, small business owners who are already swamped with the daily operations of their businesses may not have the time to learn all these things and even manage their Instagram accounts.

The good thing is, Instagram marketing can be outsourced and there are thousands of individuals and companies who are now specializing in social media platforms. In addition, there are also ways to automate most tasks involved in Instagram marketing that will make your life easier. You can learn more about the outsourcing and automation process in Chapter 7.

Is Instagram Right for You?

We have already established the fact that Instagram is a very popular platform, and you might be missing a lot of opportunities if you are not in it yet. But like any other business decision, you should consider everything before you jump in.

Is Instagram the right channel for your online marketing? If so, what are the best strategies to market your brand on Instagram?

Sure. There are around 106 million Americans using the platform, which is a massive potential audience for you to grow, but there are pointers to consider to figure out if this channel is really suitable for your business.

What are the Age Demographics of Your Target Audience?

The main factor to consider is the fact that majority of Instagrammers are between 18 and 35 years old. Is this the ideal age range for your target audience? It makes sense for a fashion brand or a food chain to invest its resources to market on Instagram, but what if you're catering to the needs of retirees? Or what if your business mainly serves other businesses in your industry (B2B) such as IT solutions, accounting, or tax compliance?

If your target audience is not really within the age demographics of Instagrammers, this channel may not be on top of your priority platforms. This is a reality that you must carefully consider before you even sign up for an Instagram business account.

But if you have a retail brand that directly sells products to customers (B2C) or if your services primarily appeal to the younger audience, then it makes sense to build a massive presence on Instagram.

Can B2B Companies Use Instagram?

Yes, businesses that are offering products and services to other businesses can still use Instagram. The same goes for businesses that are not mainly catering to the needs of younger demographics. The key is to develop a content strategy that will effectively showcase your business or brand.

Remember, boosting sales is not the only benefit that Instagram can provide for your business. With the right strategy, you can use Instagram to share your company culture, allow exclusive access to behind-the-scene events, create an engaging platform for your employees, and many more.

You'll learn more about developing a suitable content strategy for your business in Chapter 4.

Is Your Target Audience Mobile?

You also need to understand that Instagram is a mobile app. Hence, your audience can only see and engage with your brand if they are on mobile. Usually, those on Instagram are on the go, and they tend to be younger than facebook users who often check their accounts using desktop computers.

Does Your Audience Want Your Brand on Instagram?

If your target audience is on Instagram, the next factor to consider is the possibility that they want to see your brand on the platform. Based on a research conducted by GrowEpic, the top brands on Instagram are related to retail, food, beauty, and health.

However, your success on this platform is not strictly limited to your brand. Engaging content is still key. For example, NASA is far away from these industries, but they have around 14.1 million followers and one post can garner an average of 400,000 likes. You just need to really know your audience and share photos and videos that they want to see in their Instagram news feeds.

Do You Have the Skills and Resources to Effectively Use Instagram as a Marketing Platform?

Instagram is a powerful tool that will allow you to engage with your customers if you do it right. But before you can reap the rewards of customer engagement, you need to work hard on it. Again, engaging content is key in effective Instagram marketing so you must have the resources and skills to produce photos and videos that will stir the interest of your target audience.

Remember, Instagram is predominantly a photo-sharing social media channel, so your content should be designed to fit this model. Hence, you might need to redesign your content from the ground up and make sure that your brand can still convey the right message without using too much text. Do you have the skills to comply with this requirement? If not, you may need to hire an Instagram marketer or outsource the job to an online marketing agency.

Aside from the quality of content, you should also consider quantity. You must regularly post content that asks for comments from your followers. On average, you should aim share 1-2 posts every day. Don't go beyond this limit as your followers may unfollow you for posting too often, especially if your posts are all about products.

Instagram Should Not Be Your Only Channel for Online Marketing

While Instagram can provide amazing benefits for your online marketing efforts, it should only be part of a greater marketing mix.

For example, you should not expect a big surge of online traffic from Instagram because the platform is not designed for that. Instagram engagement is more about likes and comments and not clickthroughs mainly because you can't include links to your posts. You can only direct your followers to your website on your account biography.

If you want to increase clickthroughs, you should definitely include other online marketing strategies such as Search Engine Optimization and Facebook Marketing. Also remember that just like Facebook, Instagram is also a "Pay-to-Play" platform. This is in fact among the biggest misconceptions businesses often have. Some marketers who are not familiar with the platform think that all of their followers will see their posts. Instagram's algorithm puts a limit on the number of followers who can see your content. If you want your posts to reach everyone, you have to pay for the privilege. Without boosting your post as an advertisement, only a small percentage of your followers may engage in your content.

Hence, in considering Instagram as a marketing channel for your brand, you should also consider the amount you're willing to invest in this platform.

In summary, you should consider the following factors to determine if Instagram is right for your business:

- Age Demographics of your target audience (Instagrammers are between 18 and 35 years old)
- Your target audience's device preference (Instagram is a mobile app)
- The nature or industry of your brand (Successful brands on Instagram are mainly related to food, drinks, health, beauty, retail, and lifestyle)
- Your skills and resources to regularly produce engaging content
- Your marketing mix and overall online marketing strategy

Once you have determined that your brand can take advantage of Instagram, the next step is to define your target audience and make sure that your brand is properly aligned with your customers and not the other way around.

Define Your Target Audience and Brand

Instagram is only a tool, albeit a powerful one, that you can use to market your brand online. It can bring you results as long as you use the right strategies and you are targeting the right people. It still boils down to the message of your brand, and how this message will reach the right audience that you can convert to actual paying customers.

To effectively increase brand awareness and drive sales, your marketing strategy should appeal to a specific audience. Before you even use Instagram to market your brand, you should first define your target audience and determine the marketing strategies to reach them out.

Defining your target audience will help you validate your assumptions. You might even discover that your target audience is bigger and more diverse compared to what you previously thought. This could provide your business with more opportunities but may also complicate your strategy because you may need to come up with different strategies for each persona you discover on Instagram.

But defining your target audience will generally make your life easier because it will provide you a strong foundation from which to build and promote all your content through Instagram.

Market research is a crucial step that will serve as a springboard for you to define your target audience. Aside from defining your target market, we will also explore in this chapter the importance of assessing your audience behavior and optimizing your marketing strategy.

Be More Precise In Defining Your Target Audience

Traditional marketers usually categorize consumers into groups such as:

- Women 25 to 40
- Boomer men
- Stay-at-home moms
- Millennials
- Single parents

However, these too generalized categories are no longer enough. For modern marketing, especially in the Information Age and Big Data, the old marketing demographics have now more defined categories—and customers have also increased their expectations from brands.

Hence, you should be more precise in defining your target audience or you may not see the results that you are expecting. To do this, you should ask the right questions that will help you learn more about your audience:

What is your audience's biggest pain point?

Businesses are working to serve the needs of their customers. Whether you are an online retail company hoping to deliver affordable high-quality items in less time or a mortgage broker trying to provide the best financial solutions to families, you must deeply understand what your customers want. And more often than not, the biggest wants of your customers are caused by their biggest pains, which you should identify and understand. With this comprehensive knowledge, you can better develop content that you can share on Instagram and your other marketing channels to really resonate with your target audience.

What are the usual concerns of your target audience?

You should also identify the primary concerns of your target audience. It is ideal to look at the big picture and never restrict this information in the context of what your business can offer. For example, a perfume business targeting middle-aged men discovered that its target audience are concerned with career development, school-aged kids, and finding more ways to save money. With this background information, you can develop content that you can share on Instagram and other social media marketing platforms that are built around these concerns. Showing that you know your audience and you understand their daily concerns can help you nurture the relationship and build trust.

How can your brand help your target audience?

After identifying the pain points of your target audience, you should now work on how your business can help them. You might help them in saving time or money, or you may provide them entertainment. When your brand provides specific answers, help them solve their problems, or offer helpful information, they are more likely to share your Instagram posts to their followers. Once they learn to trust your brand, they are more inclined to buy from you.

Moreover, it may also help if you can find out if your target audience strongly responds to social issues and consider if your brand must take a stand. In the past, brands are quite careful in taking a stand because businesses are afraid to alienate any of their customers. But it is now proven that loyal customers can usually outweigh the detractors.

Create Customer Personas

Creating a customer persona will allow your brand-specific strategies to develop your content, which should be built around customers. By understanding the pain points of each customer, the brand can establish a series of Instagram content that is designed to match the audience's needs. After working on your customer personas, you will have a ready template that will make it easier for you to determine which specific audience will positively respond to your Instagram content.

After creating the diverse backgrounds of your customer personas, you must be able to gain a strong grasp of your audience's behavior while they're using Instagram—find out what types of content pique their attention, what specific times they are active, and which brands they follow on the platform.

Getting a deeper understanding of this will give you an idea of a better marketing mix that goes beyond Instagram marketing. For example, if one persona is spending more time on Facebook, and another on Instagram, you already have a valuable insight to properly position your content.

Defining a reliable and large source of analysis, statistics, and data is crucial in creating an effective customer persona. You can use different platforms to gather data such as website analytics, Facebook analytics, and Google analytics.

For now, you can't rely on Instagram analytics especially if you are just starting to build your followers on Instagram. Hence, you need to find more information from other channels you're currently using.

For example, data from your website analytics is crucial if you want to gain a deeper understanding of your users, the keywords they are using to find you, and the specific pages they have visited. It is ideal to involve all people in your business who are dealing with customers, especially those who take care of customer service.

Listen to Your Target Audience

Instagram is a tool that you can use for social listening, which goes beyond keeping track and replying to comments or questions posted by your audience about your brand. Social listening can help you extract important insights from social conversations that you can use for your overall online marketing strategy.

Social media listening is a great way to gain a deeper understanding of your customer personas as well as comparing your strategies to those of your competitors. The most reliable method of collecting data is to directly ask your customers, particularly about their experience about your brand.

Once you are satisfied with the data that you have collected, and you can focus the collected data to work on the ideal three to five personal files, you can move on to the next step—actually writing down your customer persona. Below is an example of a customer persona:

The Faulkners - First Time Home Buyers

Personal Background: Middle-class family, with one child and a pet. Looking for a foot in the door to home ownership based on affordability. College graduates with planned down payment assistance coming from payments, or working professionals looking to find a more convenient home. Combined median income of $96,000.

Wishes: Upgraded kitchen and plenty of natural light; comfortable, livable home; likely to be drawn to homes with sizable backyards that provide plenty of room for gardening and space for children to play.

These buyers generally want at least two bedrooms and two full bathrooms to accommodate expanding families and room for company to stay.

Challenges: Affordability and limited choices for homes

Values job security, family, better commute, discount from down payment

Biggest objection: High-interest rates, lending fees, and other hidden charges

Uses email, phone, social media (Facebook, Instagram, Twitter)

This customer persona is used by an actual mortgage broker. With this background information, the business has already identified its target audience and build content based on the persona's values and challenges. For example, the Faulkners may easily respond to Instagram posts that revolve around job security, lifestyle, value for money, and home design inspirations.

A customer persona template should be a breathing document that must be updated when necessary. Defining your target audience is not a one-time approach because you need to constantly check if the personas are still relevant to your brand. You may need to retarget your audience if you are not getting the expected results from your customer personas.

Spy on Your Competitors

When you are working on your strategy for Instagram marketing, it can be easy for marketers to think they know everything about the brand. After all, you might have spent a lot of time and resources understanding your own niche.

However, you also need to understand your market and get to know the competition. Before you start your Instagram marketing campaign, you should visit your competitor's IG profiles to know what you're up against. Assess their posts and try to make a smart guess on the demographics of their target audience.

In the process of defining your target audience, watching your competitors is crucial to ensure that your posts will stand out. If you keep spying on the actions of your competitors, you will easily know when it is time to level up so you're ahead of the game. If it will take you days or even weeks before you realize that your competitors are rolling out a marketing campaign on IG, the delay in your response could be the difference between your success and failure.

You can monitor your competitor's audience engagement on Instagram to see how they react to certain posts. This is even useful to validate if you are catering to the same audience because there's no sense wasting resources in trying to combat a non-competitor.

You can even use Instagram to look for competitors that you are not aware of. Chances are, many of your target customers on Instagram are already following brands that are offering similar products or services. Check on a specific profile of your target audience and click the brands that they are following. Browse through the list and look for brands that might be a competitor. Search for business accounts that are active on Instagram, regularly engage with their audience, and offer the products or services in your niche.

Find Your Target Audience Using Instagram Tactics

Once you are confident that you already defined your target audience, the next step is to use Instagram to find actual profiles who are within the parameters of your customer personas. Below are the top effective tactics you can use so you can search for your ideal Instagram followers.

Basically, you can use hashtags on Instagram to search for your niche, customer hobbies or interests, and industry events. While there is no geographical limit for Instagram marketing, you can use hashtags to find communities and niche groups that are relevant to your brand. Instagram has updated its algorithm to make the hashtags more discoverable for businesses.

Find the top hashtags within your niche so you can use them to achieve visibility for your ideal followers. This may take some time and effort from your end, but using relevant and popular hashtags can help you achieve your expected results. Again, you can spy on your competitors and figure out what hashtags they are using. Instagram also has a search feature that you can use to look for keywords and keyphrases.

Meanwhile, you can use hashtags to find events that are related to your industry or niche. For example, if your target audience is mainly composed of women who are interested in buying organic beauty products, you can search and follow hashtags related to this niche. Instagrammers who are using these hashtags most likely fit into your customer personas.

Aside from events, you can also use hashtags that are related to your audience's hobbies and interests. If you are promoting boho fashion items follow tags that are related to fashion such as #bohostyle, #bohochic, #bohoclothing, and other related tags. If you are a financial coach, you should follow hashtags related to finance such as #moneysavings #financialtips, #money, etc.

Another Instagram feature that you should use is location tagging. This is helpful if you are operating in specific locations. For example, if you are selling vintage clothing in New York, you should try to find audiences that are using hashtags related to #vintage and are also located in #newyork or #NY.

Remember, it takes hard work to find your target audience on Instagram. You may not see significant results in the first few weeks, so the best thing to do is to follow the strategies above and put some effort on engagement. You will eventually gain momentum.

Also, take note that this is only the beginning of your Instagram marketing efforts. In the succeeding chapters, we will discuss more strategies that will help you achieve your marketing goals.

Develop a Content Strategy

Only a few years ago, the social media world was dominated by Facebook, Twitter, and LinkedIn. But today, Twitter and LinkedIn no longer hold the rank as they were already replaced by YouTube and Instagram.

Instagram really hits the spot when it comes to being culturally relevant in comparison to YouTube and Facebook. The relatively young social media network has become one of the best places for content producers, influencers, and celebrities to share content and engage with their followers.

In Facebook, content is completely defined by the algorithm so every user receives customized content. On the other hand, the content on YouTube is usually discovered through search with less focus on the individual feed. But for Instagram, the content is sorted. There is also less noise so content producers can easily engage with their followers.

To become a long-lasting business, your brand should be part of cultural conversations that are happening online. To do this, you need to take a tailored-fit approach to developing your content strategy.

Finding Your Visual Voice

Your profile on Instagram should have a well-defined visual appeal—a consistent look and feel of content, which embodies the messages that support the goals of your business and the values of your target audience. You may use a different approach, but so far this standard for content has proven to be successful.

One great example of an Instagram profile is Califia Farm, which has more than a hundred thousand followers.

califiafarms   Follow   ▼   ...

2,295 posts   105k followers   2,171 following

Califia Farms The new shape of dairy free. Now available in: US CA (
with #CalifiaFarms
linktr.ee/califiafarms

Instagram is the perfect platform to showcase the attractive packaging of this natural beverage product that won awards in the global packaging design category from the Beverage World Magazine. The brand is consistent with its content that features the curvy bottle, whether it's the main subject of the image or more of a supplementary element in the subject of a healthy, active lifestyle that embodies the brand's customer persona.

You may say that it can be easy for B2C brands such as Califia Farm to become successful in Instagram because their products have the natural mass appeal. However, there are also B2B brands that are now making a name in the Instagram world.

For example, the Instagram account of Wells Fargo—a banking company is full of vibe that you can easily forget that it is a banking company.

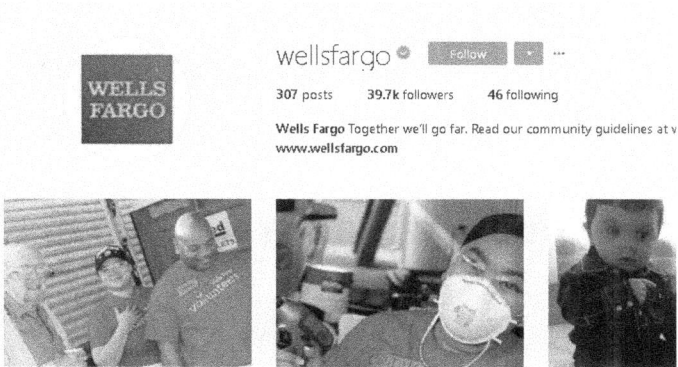

wellsfargo

307 posts   39.7k followers   46 following

Wells Fargo Together we'll go far. Read our community guidelines at v www.wellsfargo.com

Despite having only around 300 posts, the brand has already attracted 11,000 followers and counting. Its content combines a great mix of images and video that add variety to the profile. The brand also keeps its content updated and diverse by featuring different topics such as fun facts, quotes, financial tips, and current events.

There are three important elements that you need to understand to help you find your visual voice:

- Brand Values - What does your brand stands for
- Goals - What are your goals for using Instagram as a marketing platform
- Content - What are the types of content that can easily stir the interest of your target audience

When you find the right approach to creating content that covers the three elements above, you can easily attract followers and achieve your marketing goals.

What are your Instagram Marketing Goals?

Establishing clear goals for using Instagram as a marketing channel is crucial to the success of your content strategy. Defining your goals will make it easy for you if you have already achieved them. By setting metrics for your Instagram campaigns, you can easily know what posts can resonate with your target audience and what posts you should avoid.

It is also crucial to make sure that your marketing goals are achievable. For example, if you are a small flower shop in a small suburb, it can be quite unrealistic to aim for millions of followers. Try to establish a more practical goal by looking at your business operation and checking the performance of your competitors on Instagram.

In setting up your marketing goals, be sure to be as specific as you can. Avoid generic goals such as "get more followers". Rather, you could say "We have to get 500 followers each month." With this, it can be easier to know if you have achieved your goal.

What Does Your Brand Stand For?

This question can be tricky to answer especially if you are a startup. It can be easier if you already have a mission statement. Be sure to determine the unique selling point of your company. Califia Farms mainly offers the new shape of dairy free. Wells Fargo believes in community involvement as embodied on its slogan, "Together we'll go far." This is an important step in defining your content strategy so don't take shortcuts. Be certain that your brand really stands for something that you can express through Instagram. This will make it easy for you to find your visual voice and produce content that's more likely to resonate with your target audience.

What are the Types of Content that can Easily Stir the Interest of Your Target Audience?

A well-defined customer persona is crucial in developing content that can really resonate with your target audience. The specific challenges and values of your persona can help you produce content that they will actually read or watch. If possible, you can interview prospects or customers in developing your persona. Be sure to ask them about the brands they follow and who are the influencers they like to see in their feeds.

Maybe you can find a starting point by trying a popular and generic interest of your customer persona. For example, if you are a fashion brand, you can try #fashion. Try searching it on Instagram and then follow the trail by using related hashtags. Do you want to reach an audience that is interested in boho fashion?

Then try #bohofashion or #bohochick.

#fashion

500,653,203 posts

Top Posts

#bohofashion

708,401 posts

Top Posts

#bohochick

65,993 posts

Top Posts

 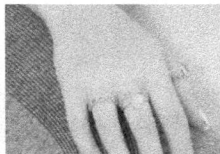 

Take a look at the Top Posts for every hashtag. Save images that you find appealing, so you can assess it later. Visit the owners of the images and make a list of influencers that you think could stir the interest of your target audience.

Visit the accounts that have garnered the highest number of followers and evaluate their content, including the hashtags they are using and stories they are posting. If you are a marketing executive, you can use this as market research for your presentation, or if you are a small business owner, you can do this on a regular basis so you can somehow learn what resonates with your persona.

You may imitate the content you see but make sure to combine it with your brand and consider your marketing goals.

It may take a while before you finally understand what is working if you just post random images you like. Still, it's not a bad idea to start posting because it will get your engines going—you'll start learning the platform and generate important insights that you can assess to better understand your target audience. However, conducting your research first is a more strategic approach.

Consider Your Business Location

Another strategy that you may do in developing content for your Instagram profile is through location audit. Try searching the locations that are crucial to your brand or target audience. This is important if you have physical outlets. Look for your locations and see what people are posting about.

Probably your target audience likes to hang out at physical locations such as the Haru Restaurant and Sushi Bar in New York City. Use at these physical locations to your market research mix so you can better understand your target market.

harusushinyc Follow

1,274 posts   7,012 followers   837 following

Haru Sushi Striking designs. Inventive menus. Sushi bars and lou ow.ly/sF0d30jh2x4

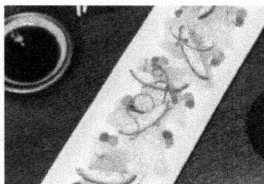

Check Your Competitors

Your brand should stand out in the market so copying your competition is a big no-no. However, you can learn a lot from your competitors and your target audience if you keep an eye on their Instagram account.

Once you have identified your competitors, search them on Instagram and check the kinds of content they are posting, the influencers they are working with, the hashtags they are using, etc. With this, you can learn more about the types of content that can really resonate with your audience without the need to experiment with your posts.

Be Consistent with Your Content

After building a profile of the type of content that you think could really work, begin testing combinations of posts that could cover the three elements of finding your visual voice: brand values, goals, and content. Be sure that you put a lot of effort into developing original content and continuously assess the followers you are attracting if they are really your target audience.

It's best to take a growth mindset in developing your content strategy and test the various forms of content. Take every opportunity to learn from your post and use insights to optimize your content, maximizing the posts that gain more engagement and avoiding posts that are not helping with your brand. This takes some time and effort until you can finally attract the audience that you really want.

Create a Calendar for Instagram Content

Creating a calendar is an ideal strategy to plan your content on Instagram. It can be overwhelming to create content that will resonate with your target audience and can really represent your brand. Hence, you must have a way to organize your content and work on a schedule that is ideal for your business. The work can be less daunting if you have a content calendar that you can use.

The primary goal of creating a content calendar for Instagram is to essentially help you in developing your content strategy. With this simplified tool, you can organize the way you create and curate content for your target audience.

With an Instagram calendar, you can cut down extra time from your content strategy that will allow you to wisely allocate your resources. This will help you in ensuring that your brand will constantly publish high-quality, high-performing, and well-written posts.

Grow Your Instagram Following

Attracting more followers on your Instagram profile can mean a stronger community for your brand, more traffic back to your website, and more sales for your business. But despite curating high-quality images and posting well-written posts, there is no guarantee that content alone can attract the right audience for your business.

In this chapter, we will explore the different tactics in making sure that your Instagram profile will gain a massive following.

Be Faithful to Your Content Strategy

Ideally, your target followers should get a good idea of what your brand is really all about within a few seconds of visiting your profile. Your posts should tell you what you really care for and what you could offer for your audience who are looking for the same images in their feeds in the future.

When we follow a specific profile on Instagram, we already have established our expectations based on our interests and passion. If you follow an account and you see a lot of nice jewelry, you are expecting to see more of it along with other cool ways to pair these aesthetics with fashionable dresses. If you follow a profile with a lot of travel pictures, you might expect to see more of it along with great recommendations for tourist spots. Now try to imagine following a boho profile and then all of a sudden they share gothic images. That is a total mismatch. There's a big chance that you may unfollow that profile.

Likewise, if your target audience follows you, they are expecting to see more of what you are posting on your profile. So if your visual voice talks about vintage fashion, keep the vintage purses, chiffon dresses, and pearls coming. This doesn't mean you can't curate images of other things, but if vintage fashion is your niche, be faithful to it and create content revolving this topic. Posting punk fashion may disappoint your target audience who are expecting a more classic and sophisticated style.Your target audience must easily be able to know your posts when they see it in their feeds.

Use the Power of Hashtags

Using hashtags is a great tactic you can use to make certain that your content will reach people who may likely follow you. And with the volume of images being uploaded every day to the platform, you really need to use hashtags for your niche so you can stand out. Generic hashtags such as #fashion #style

#love are very popular so your posts may easily get lost in the millions of photos with the same hashtag. The key is to really find the right hashtags for your brand.

To do this, you have to take some time to see the types of hashtags being used by leading profiles in your niche. Obviously, Instagram profiles with good following are using specific strategies that bring great visibility. If you found specific hashtags, determine the number of posts for each hashtag (including the top 9 grid).

For example, Coca Cola's #shareacoke campaign was among the best practices in Instagram marketing. Same with Calvin Klein's #MyCalvins.

You can add 30 hashtags on Instagram posts, and it is ideal if you could maximize this space. But there are instances when the hashtags could clutter the caption. As a workaround, you can add them as a comment. Just make sure to use '. . . . .' or a dot for every line so the comment will be truncated.

Adding hashtags can be time-consuming, so another tactic you can use is to save the hashtags you normally use into different categories so that you can just copy the right set of hashtags you want to include.

It is best to use a combination of niche and popular hashtags. If you use niche types with fewer images, there's a big chance that they will be featured in the top 9 grid, which will greatly help your brand to be discovered and attract more followers.

Join the Instagram Stories Bandwagon

Instagram Stories is one of the most effective tools for attracting a massive following. This will provide your followers a sneak peek into your brand, the people behind your team, and it also increases engagement to record heights. Instagrammers like to see raw and real posts, so be sure to post stories that are not too formal or salesy without compromising your content strategy.

Another great thing about using Instagram Stories is that you can gain an advantage if your stories are featured in the Explore Tab (the stories that you can see at the top of the page). These stories are selected by Instagram's algorithm based on the type of content that you often interact with. More often than not, these are the profiles that you don't follow, but still, they are posting the type of content that you are likely to engage with. Hence, if you have been viewing posts that are related to herbal medicine, you will see a lot of Stories featuring this niche.

When you make your stories really engaging and you regularly post high-quality content, Instagram will often feature you in the Explore tab. This may bring you a lot of followers!

Engagement Over Volume

In any social media channel, the volume of your followers will be useless if the engagement is low. You should set your strategy in a way that it will encourage your followers to interact with your content.

The quality of your followers is a crucial element in Instagram marketing. A brand with 1,000 followers who are regularly engaging with your content is far more valuable compared to a brand with 100,000 random followers composed of people who are not all qualified to be your target audience. You should attract followers who can resonate with your posts, so they can share them and interact with your online community.

In addition, the reach of your audience is an important element to consider—more than the number of your followers. For instance, even if you only have 1,000 followers on Instagram, you can gain a bigger audience if the majority of these followers are influencers in the social network.

Use the Recommended Image Size for Instagram

Using the ideal size for your Instagram images will substantially improve the aesthetic appeal of your feed, which could translate to more followers. Take note that the standard image size for Instagram is 1080 px by 1080 px. This is different from the previous standard Instagram post of 612 px by 612 px.

Instagram had to upgrade its platform so the app could keep up with high-resolution displays for advanced handheld devices. Aside from using the ideal size, you should also make certain that your posts are visually appealing. Studies suggest that brighter images attract 600 percent more likes compared to those with darker filters. Interestingly, muted palettes also tend to attract more likes, so you must use grays, blues, and greens.

Hold Instagram Promos

Holding Instagram-exclusive promos, contests, and events can significantly boost not only the number of your followers but also your engagement. Despite the many advances in the modern world, customers are still attracted to freebies and giveaways.

Just be sure that your promos will result in more followers or could improve engagement. In addition, your promo mechanics should be clear, and you should be specific on how you want your followers to participate in the promo.

Below are some examples of contests on Instagram:

1. Tag friends - Your followers can qualify to participate in the contest if they tag two or three of

their Instagram friends in the comment area of the contest picture

2. Hashtag contests - Your audience can share their own pictures by adding a contest-centric hashtag to the picture to become eligible for the contest.

3. Liking and commenting - Followers can qualify for the contest just by liking the photo specified for the contest

If you also want to increase brand awareness, you may offer your product as the prize. Also, remember to use a hashtag when you are holding a contest so that you can easily monitor the progress of the event.

As a recap, you can do the following to increase the number of your Instagram followers:

- Develop a solid content strategy and stick to it
- Embrace the power of hashtags (be sure to combine niche and popular ones)
- Maximize your exposure with Instagram Stories
- Prioritize follower engagement and quality over volume
- Use the current standard image size for your pictures (1080 px by 1080 px)
- Hold Instagram-exclusive contests

Using Instagram to Gain Sales

Some business owners and marketing executives may view Instagram as nothing more but a mobile app that you can use to showcase fancy photos. But the reality is, you can use this emerging social media platform to boost your sales.

In this chapter, we will explore specific strategies that you can apply to help you fulfill the purpose of Instagram marketing—generating sales.

Use High-Quality Images

Yep, here we go again. We need to emphasize the importance of posting high-quality images for your Instagram profile because it is the essence of effective Instagram marketing.

This is beyond the nature of Instagram as a visual-centric platform. It boils down to how our brain is rewired to better absorb visual images. Research from *Wishpond.com* reveals that 90% of information transmitted to the brain is visual, which is processed 60,000 times faster compared to written text.

Therefore, any information you may want to share with your audience can be better communicated in image form. And the quality of visuals seems to affect customer decision. Based on a survey conducted by Buffer, 67% of respondents say detailed images strongly influence their purchase decision.

Without visually-appealing images, increasing sales through Instagram can become a tedious goal to achieve. You can make this easier if you make sure that your images are of high-quality and can really resonate with your target audience.

In some instances, Instagram images that look like they are user-generated or organic tend to perform better compared to those that are too salesy or formal. However, you should still make sure that your Instagram photos are of high-quality.

Leverage Your Growing Fanbase

Another proven method of generating sales is to establish a fanbase of engaged followers—organically, of course. While this may take some time and effort on your end, it is easier to promote your products and services if you have well-targeted followers on Instagram.

Increasing your sales through Instagram is the culmination of the strategies and tactics we have explored in the previous chapters—from defining your target audience, developing your content strategy, and growing your Instagram following. If done right, these steps can significantly help attract organic followers that you may convert into customers or even advocates or brand ambassadors.

But if you really want to speed up the process of generating sales, there are specific budget-driven strategies you can explore: Instagram Ads and Influencer Marketing.

Instagram Ads

Advertising on Instagram can help you promote your products and services by encouraging potential customers to visit your website. You can design your sponsored ads in a way that you can send people to important sections of your website, usually the sections that will help you sell your products or services.

Moreover, you can also design your Instagram ads to boost website conversion. With this, you can get people to take specific actions on your website such as buy products, sign up for a membership, subscribe to a newsletter, and more.

Aside from attracting website visitors, Instagram ads can also help you increase mobile app installations, boosting mobile app engagement. Meanwhile, businesses can also achieve predictable reach and greater control over message frequency.

Finally, you can use Instagram ads to promote mass awareness to a broader audience with guaranteed impressions and placement in the top ad position of Instagram's feed.

Like with other forms of online marketing, it's ideal to do some experiments to determine which content works best.

Hence, you need to try different types of content (images, videos, gif, boomerang) as part of your Instagram marketing strategy. Just be certain that you are keeping track of your numbers to monitor the performance of your Instagram ads. With this, you can intensify your efforts on ads that are working and cease the ads that are not bringing the expected results. Once you become familiar with Instagram posts, you may need to experiment with various ad formats.

Pay Instagram Influencers

Another option to quickly boost your sales through Instagram is to pay for influencers on the platform to promote your brand. You may choose to pay influencers to promote your Instagram profile or a photo with a link that will direct your audience to your landing pages.

The link for the second option should redirect your potential customers to a landing page where they can buy your products. The key to this strategy is to find influencers who have thousands of followers and then enter into a short-term sponsorship deal, which only includes one to two posts during the initial phase.

Long-term sponsorship is not ideal if you are just starting with this strategy. It will cost you more if you like to pay for more endorsement posts. Meanwhile, keeping endorsement posts for even a week is not usually worth it as posts on Instagram have the tendency to gain less reach with age.

Make sure that you are using high-quality images that are not too salesy as these tend to resonate well with Instagrammers. Formal and straightforward content may also fail to appeal to people who are using Instagram as a form of pastime.

There are three important pointers that you should bear in mind for influencer marketing on Instagram.

First, you must be certain that the landing page you want your customers to visit is properly optimized for conversion. You may attract people through influencers, but if your landing page is not well optimized, your efforts could be put to waste. Ideally, your landing page should convert visitors into actual customers.

Second, you should be open for experiments. While there are strategies and tactics that are proven effective, you still need to test them out if they can bring the expected results for your brand. There's no surefire way to know what can work until you try the approaches you have learned in this book. Thus, you need to try varying images and copies when you want to connect with your target audience. You may also need to try different types of influencers with different audiences to check how your offer can convert to another market segment. On top of that, you should consider making different offers as this could affect lead conversions.

Third, you have to closely monitor Instagram analytics. You need to keep track of the money you are spending on influencers and the profit you are getting from this tactic. Find out which influencers are bringing you results. Try to determine specific marketing qualities that make the influencers stand out compared to others. The next logical step is to look for other influencers that are offering the same marketing aspects. Don't be afraid to spend money on influencers if they can really boost your sales.

It's All about Your Mindset

It can be really exciting to use Instagram as a platform to boost your sales as long as you do it right. Often, transforming Instagram as a sales channel will require a different mindset. Basically, you have to be familiar with your audience on Instagram as well as the type of content that can stir their interest.

Remember, Instagram is a visual-centric social media platform, so you need to learn how to produce images that can resonate well with your audience.

Whether you pay influencers to promote your brand, organically grow your profile, or buy ads, there are many effective ways to boost sales through Instagram.

Outsourcing Your Instagram Account

Giant brands such as Adidas, Coca-Cola, and Victoria's Secret have the resources to outsource their Instagram activities to top digital agencies, so their people can focus more on other important aspects of the business. However, even startups and small and medium enterprises (SMEs) can still outsource their social media, especially Instagram.

Whether you choose to outsource social media to a freelance consultant or to an external agency, you can easily free important hours you can use to manage and grow your business. But before you take the plunge, there are several important things that you need to consider.

Benefits of Outsourcing Instagram Marketing

At this point, you should be already aware of the fact that Instagram can help your business in many ways. You can take advantage of Instagram to engage your target audience if your business is active in their conversations. The more you post on Instagram, the more results you can expect. This requires time, at least one hour every day, to monitor your Instagram channel, share high-quality content, engage with your audience, and nurture your brand in the process.

If you own a small business, your time is mainly devoted to operations and business development. It can be difficult to find the required time to build your Instagram strategy, implement best practices, and monitor the results. And this is only for one channel. What if you also want to gain presence on other social media platforms like Facebook, Twitter, LinkedIn, or Pinterest?

This is the reason why outsourcing your social media activity to an expert agency or professional is often worthwhile.

Key Qualities to Look For

If you are ready to narrow down the list of qualified agencies or freelancers, you need to make sure that they have the following important qualities:

- Know-how of how Instagram works from a business perspective. While anyone can use Instagram, not everyone has the knowledge and the expertise to use it as a tool to grow a business. You should look for a freelancer or an agency who knows how to drive activity on the platform to help you achieve your goals for your brand.
- Enthusiasm for Instagram. Being an Instagrammer doesn't instantly make someone an expert on the platform.

It is ideal to work with someone who has a genuine passion for the job. It takes commitment not just to be constantly active on social media, but to keep up with the ever-changing nature of social media marketing.

- Multiple skills. Instagram marketing requires a lot of skills. You need someone who has good aesthetic sense, can write concise yet compelling captions, can analyze data and provide you with relevant business insights, and can engage with your followers.

- Creativity. This is an important quality that your Instagram manager should possess. Instagram is a wonderful tool that can really bring your business to greater heights if you are creative enough. Look for a manager who is curious, has a sense of humor, and knows how to think outside the box.

- Ask for previous work. There's no better way of knowing whether he's qualified than to assess the previous work of your Instagram manager. This will provide you the opportunity to assess the results that the candidate can bring to the table.

What are the Things You Can Outsource to an Instagram Manager?

Instagram marketing is beyond sharing a few posts when you feel like it. Below are endeavors that any good Instagram manager should be able to handle:

- Instagram strategy - This includes identifying your target audience, posting frequency, types of content, influencer marketing, and more
- Instagram setup and branding - As we have discussed in the previous chapters, it is crucial that your Instagram profile has a consistent visual voice
- Content marketing - Developing original Instagram content that can resonate well with your target audience
- Audience engagement - Joining conversations with your current followers to answer queries or share information about your brand
- Instagram monitoring - Activating the radar for mentions of your brand and engaging with these mentions
- Influencer marketing - Finding possible influencers who can promote your brand on Instagram

It is best to look for a freelancer or an agency that is familiar with your niche or your industry. Often, these people are also willing to handle your other social media marketing channels.

How to Get Started with an Instagram Manager

Most freelance marketing consultants and digital agencies will ask to review your Instagram profile if you already have one and will provide recommendations based on your business goals. Usually, you need to discuss your target audience, current marketing strategy or campaigns you have implemented in the past for Instagram, your budget for ads, and other important matters.

Your Instagram manager will probably recommend concentrating on several strategies first, so you can try which one is working for your business.

In outsourcing, you have to keep your external consultant updated of important business information so they can plan properly. You have to inform them about new or discontinued products, events you may be attending, special promos or contests you have in mind, changes to company rules, or any update on your customer service policies.

Where to Find an Instagram Manager

Social media marketing, especially Instagram management, is a rising job opportunity, so you can easily find a freelancer or a digital agency that can take care of your online profile. You may ask referrals from your business connections or ask local groups to see if they can recommend agencies or freelancers.

Of course, you can use social media networks such as Twitter and LinkedIn to look for people and companies offering Instagram management services. There are also job marketplaces where you can post such as Upwork, Credo, and Outsourcely to find freelancers.

Conclusion

There are three important pointers that you need to remember for effective Instagram marketing.

First, you must be sure that the content you share through Instagram will reflect the values that you represent as a brand. Being genuine can help you resonate well with your target audience.

Second, you should be flexible without compromising your business goals. Even though the strategies and tactics described in this book are proven effective, you must still be open to experimenting to see which can really bring results.

Third, you should always be mindful of your Instagram activities. While you can outsource the job, it is still your responsibility to make sure that your posts are beneficial to your brand and your activities can bring results. Be on top of your online activities as it can make or break your business.

I hope this book was able to help you understand the magic of using Instagram as a tool to grow your business. Thank you again for downloading this book!

www.ingramcontent.com/pod-product-compliance
Lightning Source LLC
Chambersburg PA
CBHW071516210326
41597CB00018B/2777